POWER
WALK

DEVOTIONAL JOURNAL

• •

40 DAY JOURNEY TO POWER

• •

KARREN D. TODD

Power Walk by Karren D. Todd
www.powerwalk.online
Copyright 2017 © Karren D. Todd

ISBN: 978-0-692-67774-2

First Printing

Printed in the United States of America

Devotional Layout: Dion Paul
Book Cover Design: JoVenTosh www.brandyoubrandnu.com

DEDICATION

This devotional is dedicated to my parents, Bobby and Alice Todd.

My Dad who always encouraged me to walk with power and my Mom –
who introduced me to Christ- and whose transition in 2012 increased my
desire for discipline in my devotion time.

They are the springboard from which I jump…

Special thanks to everyone who laid eyes on this devotional
(over a three year period) before it reached the hands of the public:
Joyce McKinney, Sharon Avery Smith, Arnita Fields, Brandi Hunter &
Dion Paul.

Your contributions to the effort do not go unnoticed – even if they went
unpaid…

INTRODUCTION

POWER W A L K

Before I became a runner (and I still use that term loosely) I started my exercise journey with a daily power walk. Each morning I would force myself out of bed and hit the pavement because I wanted to be a better me. Just as you exercise physically you also need spiritual exercise to increase your endurance, your faith and your passion to be who God created you to be. Power Walk is a 40 day devotional journey that uses real talk to shake you from your bed of contentment, support you with God's Word and inspire you to walk with POWER!

THIS IS HOW IT WORKS:

Each day you will train in three areas on your Power Walk.
First, there is WISDOM. This short reading wakes you up, opens your heart & prepares you to receive the revelation that God has for you.

Second, there is the WORD. There are one or more scriptures for each day that inspire and support the "real talk" wisdom. Always remember: God's word is a seed planted in your hearts & in your spirits to help you to grow into the woman of faith that God has designed you to be.

Third, there is **WORK**. You will read and respond to journal questions. Spend honest time with yourself as you reflect on and answer these questions. Do the work. And as you allow the interactivity of God's Word and YOUR work to consistently become an important part of your day, you will see the power of God increase in your life.

LET'S PRACTICE

First, the WISDOM:

He's already forgiven what you can't forget. Stop playing your sin movie over and over in your head. You can still have a happy ending even though you're not living a fairy tale.

Then, the WORD:

...as far as the east is from the west, so far has he removed our transgressions from us. (Psalm 103:12 NIV84)

Now, it's time to do the WORK:

In this section you will answer introspective questions to move you forward.

**Is there something in your past that you have not forgiven yourself for? What scripture and positive thoughts can you use to replace the pain of unforgiveness that lingers in your mind and heart? Commit to repeating the scriptures and positive thoughts each time you are reminded of your past failures.

Remember to ALWAYS answer the questions. This is where you connect and apply God's truth to your life. When you apply God's truth the result is God's POWER! I am excited about your journey.

Your POWER WALK starts now...

DAY ONE

··

What will you do differently today that will move you closer to where you want to be?

··

<u>*THE WISDOM*</u>*:*

You've been feeling like God is blessing everybody but you. You see other people moving forward and you're wondering if it will ever be your turn. You try not to complain because you know you did your dirt in the past. Let me encourage you. What you did in your past has not disqualified you from your future.

My prayer for you today is that you stop allowing the enemy to make you feel useless and stuck. That's a trick to make you believe that God's promises are not for you. **YOU DID NOT MISS YOUR "ONLY" CHANCE.** God still sees you. God still loves you. God still has plans for you. The detour you took in your past caused a delay but it has not caused a denial. I'm praying for you and I'm excited about your future!

<u>*THE WORD*</u>*:*

For I know the plans I have for you," declares the Lord, "plans to prosper you and not to harm you, plans to give you hope and a future. (Jeremiah 29:11 NIV84)

<u>*DAY ONE - THE WORK*</u>:

- *Name one goal you want to accomplish in five years or less.*

- *Name one thing you will do differently today that will move you closer to where you want to be.*

_____

_____

_____

_____

_____

_____

_____

_____

_____

_____

_____

_____

_____

_____

_____

_____

_____

_____

D A Y   T W O

....

There is a difference in living to please
*people and living to **serve** people.*

....

<u>*THE WISDOM:*</u>

God has a purpose for you, but sometimes it doesn't match what everyone else says is *"best"* for you. Live your life so that you can stand before
God without shame or regret. Walk in your purpose. Those who don't
believe or support you can catch up with you later. **IT'S YOUR TIME!**

....

<u>*THE WORD:*</u>

So then, each of us will give an account of himself to God. (Romans 14:12
NIV84)

....

DAY TWO - THE WORK:

- *Do you live more to please people or serve people?*

- *Name one thing you keep putting on the back burner because you don't think others will "get it."*

- *What can you do today to overcome people-pleasing and walk into your purpose?*

_____

_____

_____

_____

_____

_____

_____

_____

_____

_____

_____

_____

_____

_____

DAY THREE

••

If God has shown you your divine purpose, that's a blessing.

••

THE WISDOM:

If you don't know yet, that's ok. Find purpose in or add purpose to what you are doing now. There is a reason you are where you are. Fulfill **TO-DAY'S** purpose and stop being anxious about what's next or what *God* showed you. It's all about timing. Calm down. God has not forgotten the plans He has for you. You can't get to **LATER** if you give up **NOW**.

•••

THE WORD:

For I know the plans I have for you," declares the Lord, "plans to prosper you and not to harm you, plans to give you hope and a future. (Jeremiah 29:11 NIV84)

And let us not be weary in well doing: for in due season we shall reap, if we faint not. (Galatians 6:9 KJV)

•••

DAY THREE - THE WORK:

- *If you don't feel as if you are operating in your purpose, how can you add purpose to what you are already doing?*

- *How can you be God's representative in your current situation?*

- *Name one way that you can combat the anxiety of NOW as you press toward your LATER.*

_____

_____

_____

_____

_____

_____

_____

_____

_____

_____

_____

_____

_____

_____

D A Y   F O U R

Was that God talking or was that you?

THE WISDOM:

Sometimes it's hard to tell the difference. Your thoughts are so loud and emotions so strong that they are drowning out the *whisper* of God. Because of that, you have stayed too long in the wrong place or moved to the new place too soon.

My prayer for you today is that God sharpens your discernment and opens your heart to the promptings of the Holy Spirit; that you know with **CONFIDENCE** that the small whisper you heard saying, 'STOP', 'GO', 'YES', or 'NO', was the *voice of God*.

THE WORD:

Whether you turn to the right or to the left, your ears will hear a voice behind you, saying, "This is the way; walk in it." (Isaiah 30:21 NIV84)

DAY FOUR - THE WORK:

- *What habit have you carried for so long that you've accepted it as a part of you – but it needs to change?*

- *What or who do you need to separate yourself from so that you can hear God's voice with clarity?*

_____

_____

_____

_____

_____

_____

_____

_____

_____

_____

_____

_____

_____

_____

_____

DAY FIVE

....

God is able to deliver *so it frustrates us when He doesn't.*

....

THE WISDOM:

However, if God *always* delivered you immediately, you would have no need for faith and you would never learn to *trust* Him. The situation you're going through is not out of control; it's just out of **YOUR** control.

My prayer for you today is that instead of being anxious about 'when' and 'how much longer' – you find peace in knowing that He's with you right now during your valley experience. God doesn't just show up with the promise, He walks with you (or even carries you) through the process. Keep trusting. God is going to do what He said.

....

THE WORD:

Even though I walk through the valley of the shadow of death, I will fear no evil, for you are with me; your rod and your staff, they comfort me. (Psalm 23:4 NIV84)

....

DAY FIVE - THE WORK:

- *Name something God has delivered you from in the past.*

- *How can you use that experience to increase your faith during your current situation?*

- *Is there anything you can do today that will help to bring peace to your mind and spirit during this valley experience?*

_____

_____

_____

_____

_____

_____

_____

_____

_____

_____

_____

_____

_____

_____

DAY SIX

....

Jesus is a burden lifter not a burden snatcher.

....

THE WISDOM:

He won't take what you won't give. So why not take the pain from your past or the problems in your present and *release* them into the hands of the Master? Some stuff and some people you can't fix! You're only making it worse.

That situation, that relationship, the same dumb stuff over and over has burned you to a crisp. There are places in your heart where only ashes remain. My prayer for you today is that you stop holding on to the ugliness of your past. Release it and trust Him with your ashes. God has beauty waiting for you.

....

THE WORD:

...and provide for those who grieve in Zion— to bestow on them a crown of beauty instead of ashes, the oil of gladness instead of mourning, and a garment of praise instead of a spirit of despair. (Isaiah 61:3a NIV84)

....

DAY SIX - THE WORK:

- *Name an issue you are dealing with that you need to release to God because it is beyond your control.*

- *How have you made it worse than it was in the beginning?*

- *Name one thing you can change in your behavior that will let God know you are releasing this issue to Him.*

_____

_____

_____

_____

_____

_____

_____

_____

_____

_____

_____

_____

_____

_____

_____

DAY SEVEN

....

Your attitude is jacked up.

....

THE WISDOM:

You get mad too quick, cuss too much and you know it. You keep doing the same thing you said you wouldn't, repeating instead of repenting and you know it. You can do better but sometimes you don't want to. That's selfish and you know it.

What's mind blowing is that God is still blessing you and keeping you and you know it. He's still giving you grace and mercy; still keeping His promises and you know it. He's still holding up **His** end of the bargain; still waiting on you and you know it. It's time for you to start acting like you know. And you know it.

My prayer for you today is that you become a doer of what you know, not just a hearer. Your blessing is in the **DOING**! In the words of G.I. Joe, "Knowing is only half the battle."

....

THE WORD:

Do not merely listen to the word, and so deceive yourselves. Do what it says. (James 1:22 NIV84)

But the man who looks intently into the perfect law that gives freedom, and continues to do this, not forgetting what he has heard, but doing it- he will be blessed in what he does. (James 1:25 NIV84)

....

DAY SEVEN - THE WORK:

- *What repeat behaviors keep you from being fully in the will of God?*

- *How do you know this behavior offends God or is against His will?*

- *What can you do today to begin to wean yourself from your bad habits and move closer to habits that are Christ-centered?*

_____

_____

_____

_____

_____

_____

_____

_____

_____

_____

_____

_____

_____

_____

_____

_____

DAY EIGHT

••

*I know it's frustrating right now but
God is teaching you how to be disciplined.*

••

THE WORD:

He is closing doors that take you off **His** path for your life. Pay attention to the things, people, and habits that God says **NO** to in your life. It will help you to know what to say **NO** to in the future. God is not being unreasonable. He just won't release "that" to you because "that" is not yours.

My prayer for you today is that you stop kicking and screaming about what God is not doing in your life; that you stop forcing the things, opportunities and relationships He has already said **NO** to. Because what you 'think' you want is more trouble than it is or they are worth. Be patient and wait on God's **YES**. There is peace attached to God's **YES**. Trust me, you never know how valuable peace is until you don't have it anymore. I pray that the decisions you make today produce the fruit of peace in your life. And it is so, In Jesus' name.

•••

THE WORD:

No discipline seems pleasant at the time, but painful. Later on, however, it produces a harvest of righteousness and peace for those who have been trained by it. (Hebrews 12:11 NIV84)

•••

DAY EIGHT - THE WORK:

- *Are there things, people or habits that God is saying NO to in your life?*

- *How have you handled the NO?*

- *How can you better appreciate God's redirection (not rejection) in your life?*

_____

_____

_____

_____

_____

_____

_____

_____

_____

_____

_____

_____

_____

_____

DAY NINE

....

Does God love you like you are?

....

THE WISDOM:

Absolutely. Does he want you to stay like you are? Absolutely **NOT**. Stop excusing your behavior saying, "That's just how I am" and begin to *move forward* today to become who God says you are. You can do it. I believe in you.

STOP allowing the enemy to make you feel like you are failing God or that God is so disappointed with you that He no longer cares about you. I pray that every time you **START** to believe the enemy's lies, **God** *reminds* you of the truth in His Word. I speak that your *hope is restored* and today you will *receive* an abundance of peace and joy.

....

THE WORD:

May the God of hope fill you with all joy and peace as you trust in him, so that you may overflow with hope by the power of the Holy Spirit. (Romans 15:13 NIV84)

....

DAY NINE - THE WORK:

- *What behaviors or character flaws are you excusing that may be delaying your journey to your destiny?*

- *Do you feel guilty or extremely disappointed with your efforts to overcome these issues?*

- *As you trust God with these issues, what can you do today to make steps toward overcoming this behavior and any negative emotions that you have developed?*

_____

_____

_____

_____

_____

_____

_____

_____

_____

_____

_____

_____

D A Y   T E N

....

God has not given you what you're asking for because you still haven't done the last thing He told you to do.

....

THE WISDOM:

You've been so afraid of making the wrong decision that you haven't made **ANY** decisions. You are over thinking it and over analyzing it and now you have the "*paralysis of analysis*" and the enemy loves it.

You're *concentrating* so hard on staying in God's will that you're second guessing what He said. What if that wasn't God? What if that was me? Now your anxiety has lead to avoidance. *Relax.* Step out on faith. Baby, **God** can't order your steps if you're too scared to move! As long as it's not against *His word* and your motives are pure. Follow your heart. Take the leap. My God is able to keep you from falling.

THE WORD:

Cast all your anxiety on him because he cares for you. (1 Peter 5:7 NIV84)

Now all glory to God, who is able to keep you from falling away and will bring you with great joy into his glorious presence without a single fault. (Jude 1:24 NLT)

....

DAY TEN - THE WORK:

- *What was the last thing that was placed in your heart to do that you have not completed?*

- *Why haven't you completed it?*

- *Write three steps you can pray over that will remove your paralysis so that you can add feet to your faith.*

_____

_____

_____

_____

_____

_____

_____

_____

_____

_____

_____

_____

_____

_____

DAY ELEVEN

....

It's been *a long hard struggle but trust me,* *you're* closer *than you've ever been*.

....

THE WISDOM:

Don't give up. God is going to do what *He said*. The problem you're struggling with right now is not a cliffhanger. God will not leave you hanging by saying: **TO BE CONTINUED**. He will walk with you until you reach **THE END**.

I know you're tired, but you've come too far and invested too much. There is joy at the end of this. There is peace at the end of this. Your blessing is at the **END** of this but you've got to push until **THE END**. It's always darkest before the dawn but I see the dawn of your breakthrough and it's going to be worth the wait. Fight on! I'm praying for you.

....

THE WORD:

Let us not become weary in doing good, for at the proper time we will reap a harvest if we do not give up. (Galatians 6:9 NIV84)

The man said, "Let me go; it's daybreak." Jacob said, "I'm not letting you go 'til you bless me." (Genesis 32:26 MSG)

....

DAY ELEVEN - THE WORK:

- What are you waiting on God for?

- Have you been challenged in the process or felt like giving up?

- Name one way that you can increase your faith or encourage yourself.

- Name two potential prayer partners that can pray with you for endurance. Set a reminder in your phone to reach out to them today.

_____

_____

_____

_____

_____

_____

_____

_____

_____

_____

_____

_____

_____

DAY TWELVE

....
Every *decision counts.*
....

THE WISDOM:

Stop doing random stuff and 'hoping' everything will be okay. What you do today **WILL** affect your future. *Be* intentional about *your choices and your decisions.* I know tomorrow is not promised but what if tomorrow comes? Are you ready for it?

God's wisdom says invest in your physical, emotional, financial and spiritual **PRESENT** so that you can have a better tomorrow. My prayer for you today is that you *eat right, sleep right, live right and love right* so that you can enjoy tomorrow and not spend it cleaning up the mess you made yesterday.

Wisdom is choosing to do now what you will be happy with later.
--Joyce Meyer

THE WORD:

Blessed is the man who finds wisdom, the man who gains understanding,
(Proverbs 3:13 NIV84)

The wise inherit honor, but fools he holds up to shame. (Proverbs 3:35 NIV84)

DAY TWELVE - THE WORK:

- *What positive action did you take yesterday that yielded a positive result today?*

- *Did you do something negative recently that you had to reap the consequences of?*

- *How can you invest in your physical, emotional, financial and spiritual being NOW, so that you can have a better future?*

_____

_____

_____

_____

_____

_____

_____

_____

_____

_____

_____

_____

_____

_____

DAY THIRTEEN

· ·

It's hard for you to see your true value
because God is not finished with you.

· ·

THE WISDOM:

You keep looking at what you can see, but God works on the invisible before the visible; from the **inside out**. Your goal is still reachable. Your dream is still attainable. God will not go back on His word.

Life is filled with road blocks, pit stops and pot holes. Sometimes it seems that you'll never reach your destination or your full potential. My prayer for you today is that you keep the faith and allow God to finish what He started. It will all happen in **HIS** time. Stop waiting on a microwave miracle when God wants you **WELL DONE**. I know it seems like you're all over the place, but trust me. You are not just a piece of work. You are a work of art and a masterpiece that has the Master's peace.

THE WORD:

...being confident of this, that he who began a good work in you will carry it on to completion until the day of Christ Jesus. (Philippians 1:6 NIV84)

Have I not commanded you? Be strong and courageous. Do not be frightened, and do not be dismayed, for the Lord your God is with you wherever you go."
(Joshua 1:9 ESV)

Do you not know that in a race all the runners run, but only one receives the prize? So run that you may obtain it. (1 Corinthians 9:24 ESV)

It is God who arms me with strength and keeps my way secure. (Psalm 18:32 NIV)

DAY THIRTEEN - THE WORK:

- *Is there anything in your life today that is testing your faith?*

- *Is there anything that is draining your faith?*

- *How can you replenish your faith today so that you can trust God through your process?*

_____

_____

_____

_____

_____

_____

_____

_____

_____

_____

_____

_____

_____

_____

D A Y   F O U R T E E N

••

Today I pray that God stirs up the desire in you
to live a LIFE of freedom.

••

THE WISDOM:

You have been emotionally and financially bound for too long and it feels like every time you break free, something happens that pulls you or knocks you back into bondage.

My prayer for you today is that you loose the chains of your past. Chains could be people, places, or even habits that continue to creep into your present and attempt to delay your future. Today receive and celebrate God's peace, God's liberty and God's joy. Glance in your rear view mirror but **LOOK** forward out of your windshield. That's why it's bigger anyway. **Stay free!**

THE WORD:

Stand fast therefore in the liberty by which Christ has made us free, and do not be entangled again with a yoke of bondage. (Galatians 5:1 NKJV)

So if the Son sets you free, you will be free indeed. (John 8:36 NIV84)

DAY FOURTEEN - THE WORK:

- *Name the "chains" in your life that keep you from living a life of freedom that God has promised you.*

- *Separate the list by what you can control and what you cannot control.*

- *Choose one "chain" you can control and name three steps that you will take to break free from it.*

_____

_____

_____

_____

_____

_____

_____

_____

_____

_____

_____

_____

_____

_____

_____

DAY FIFTEEN

··

Don't have an **emotional reaction** *today that could change the course of your day, weekend or life.*

··

THE WISDOM:

To get to God's result *you've* got to make a *God* choice even when you don't feel like it. All of this 'clicking' and cussing people out is nothing but an adult temper tantrum. You are too old for that! *Choose* God's way.

Examine yourself and start working on *you* and your attitude. People couldn't always **"push your buttons"** if you didn't have so many of them! Now your day is ruined, your joy is nonexistent and the enemy is elated. He's not stealing your joy. You keep giving it to him. My prayer for you today is that you **guard** your emotions, **guard** your tongue and **guard** your anointing. Breathe. Stretch. Shake. Let it go.

···

THE WORD:

When words are many, sin is NOT absent, but he who holds his tongue is wise. (Proverbs 10:19 NIV84)

Watch your words and hold your tongue; you'll save yourself a lot of grief. (Proverbs 21:23 MSG)

The hotheaded do things they'll later regret... (Proverbs 14:17a MSG)

···

DAY FIFTEEN - THE WORK:

- *Which emotions do you have trouble controlling?*

- *Circle the one you will begin to work on today and find one biblical scripture that will help you stay on guard.*

_____

_____

_____

_____

_____

_____

_____

_____

_____

_____

_____

_____

_____

_____

_____

_____

DAY SIXTEEN

••

I know you don't like where you are right now.

••

THE WISDOM:

You keep trying to be strong; trying to grin and bear it and even trying to **'speak those things.'** But your heart is still broken and trying to be positive makes you feel fake. The enemy says quit lying to yourself. You are a mess. But the Holy Spirit says:

You are not a mess. This situation is just messy and God can take 'messy' and make a **MIRACLE**.

Baby, all God needs to work a miracle is a miracle situation! Although you feel like this time is worse than the last time and your heart and spirit have been broken beyond repair, I pray that you give the broken pieces to the Master. Keep trusting God for your miracle. The Potter **WANTS** to put you back together again. I'm praying for you.

••

THE WORD:

Then I went down to the potter's house, and behold, he was working at the wheel. And the vessel that he was making from clay was spoiled in the hand of the potter; so he made it over, reworking it into another vessel as it seemed good to the potter to make it. Then the word of the Lord came to me: O house of Israel, can I not do with you as this potter does? says the Lord. Behold, as the clay is in the potter's hand, so are you in My hand, O house of Israel. (Jeremiah 18:3- 6 AMP)

••

DAY SIXTEEN - THE WORK:

- Is there something in your life that is causing heartbreak or challenging your faith?

- Write down what has been broken, taken or lost.

- Now present the list to God in prayer and write down what you hear in your spirit after you pray.

_____

_____

_____

_____

_____

_____

_____

_____

_____

_____

_____

_____

_____

DAY SEVENTEEN

The power of life and death are in your tongue.

THE WISDOM:

You keep killing your own hopes, dreams and self-esteem every time you open your mouth! You talk yourself out of God's promises every day and wonder why God is not keeping up His end of the bargain. It's not Him, it's **YOU**.

You pray for breakthrough and speak *'I'll never get out of this situation'*. You pray for prosperity and speak *'I stay broke'*. My prayer for you today is that you line up your mind with the mind of Christ and fill your mouth with His word. God is waiting on you to SPEAK LIFE.

[HOMEWORK: Pay attention to what you say today - it might just show you what you REALLY believe.]

THE WORD:

He who guards his lips guards his life, but he who speaks rashly will come to ruin. (Proverbs 13:3 NIV84)

Death and life are in the power of the tongue, and they who indulge in it shall eat the fruit of it [for death or life]. (Proverbs 18:21 AMP)

DAY SEVENTEEN - THE WORK:

- *Pay attention to the negative comments or thoughts that you have today.*

- *If possible, keep a record in your phone so that you can refer back to see the areas/situations that breed negativity in your thoughts and speech.*

- *Also, spend the day wearing a rubber band and snap it every time you say something negative.*

_____

_____

_____

_____

_____

_____

_____

_____

_____

_____

_____

D A Y   E I G H T E E N

· ·

God says, "Yes, no, or not now."

· ·

THE WISDOM:

The issue is, the only answer we REALLY want is Yes. So, we *keep* praying like God is not answering us or we ask other people to join us in prayer like *'majority rules.'* Now you're spinning your wheels trying to stay where God said leave or you're out of God's will trying to go when He said **NO**.

God is *protecting you* from dangers seen and unseen. You think you can handle it but God knows best. Isn't that why you asked Him in the first place? You're not 'waiting to hear from God, you're waiting on **Him** to change and give you the answer **YOU** want. My prayer for you today is that you trust and accept God's answer for whatever you're facing right now. God has spoken and you heard Him clearly. Act accordingly. I'm praying for you.

· ·

THE WORD:

Trust in the Lord with all your heart and lean not on your own understanding; in all your ways acknowledge him, and he will make your paths straight. (Proverbs 3:5, 6 NIV84)

The eyes of the Lord are on the righteous and his ears are attentive to their cry; (Psalm 34:15 NIV84)

· ·

DAY EIGHTEEN - THE WORK:

- *Is there a situation in your life where you know you are not fully trusting God?*

- *Are your actions lining up with your faith or your understanding?*

- *Read and repeat Proverbs 3:5-6 throughout the day as you begin to trust and accept God's answers in your life.*

_____

_____

_____

_____

_____

_____

_____

_____

_____

_____

_____

_____

_____

_____

DAY NINETEEN

....

I keep hearing: RECALCULATING!

....

THE WISDOM:

I don't know what you've been **PRAYING** for but because of what you just **REPENTED** for, God has just put you back on the path to your promise.

You made the wrong decision. You chose the wrong person, place, or path. You got off on the wrong exit, but as soon as you repented God's GPS started recalculating. Be encouraged! We all make mistakes. If it was easy to live right, everyone would be doing it. The blessing is still yours. Your direction was just rerouted. My prayer is that you listen closely, pray continually and walk accordingly. God is about to bring you back! I'm excited for you!

....

THE WORD:

The Lord is not slow in keeping his promise, as some understand slowness. He is patient with you, not wanting anyone to perish, but everyone to come to repentance. (2 Peter 3:9 NIV84)

If we confess our sins, he is faithful and just and will forgive us our sins and purify us from all unrighteousness. (1 John 1:9 NIV84)

....

DAY NINETEEN - THE WORK:

- *Is there something in your life that you've been praying for but need to repent for not fully trusting God?*

- *Take the time now to ask God for forgiveness then listen closely throughout the day for any clarity or further instructions. Be prepared to write those instructions in your journal or in the notes app on your phone; you will need to refer back to them to "walk accordingly."*

_____

_____

_____

_____

_____

_____

_____

_____

_____

_____

_____

_____

_____

_____

D A Y   T W E N T Y

....

Stop excusing away the desires to do better or be better that God is planting in your spirit.

....

<u>*THE WISDOM*</u>:

God wants to finish what He started but you keep stalling. You've still got the same amount of money in savings, you're still the same weight and your dreams are still collecting dust. Stop making excuses!

You've started a million projects and haven't finished one because your creativity outweighs your commitment. You keep creating excuses instead of committing to the plan. God has not given you those desires for them to stay in your head. He's given you the desire to do better and want more because that's what He wants for you. Allow God to join you in your work because He's not going to do it all for you. The world **NEEDS** your gift! What are you doing today that leads to your dream, to your goal or to your destiny? I'm waiting but more importantly, God is waiting.

....

<u>*THE WORD*</u>:

In all my prayers for all of you, I always pray with joy because of your partnership in the gospel from the first day until now, being confident of this, that he who began a good work in you will carry it on to completion until the day of Christ Jesus. (Philippians 1:4-6 NIV84)

....

DAY TWENTY - THE WORK:

- *Today make a list of things you will FINISH (not start) in the next week or month, then put a reminder in your phone to come back to this page on that date and see what you have accomplished.*

_____

_____

_____

_____

_____

_____

_____

_____

_____

_____

_____

_____

_____

_____

DAY TWENTY-ONE

······································

*I wonder what your life would look like
if your grace ran out?*

······································

THE WISDOM:

So why are you so quick to cancel or revoke your grace with others?
No Mistakes Allowed is a song, not a way of life. This mantra should
not be your rule of thumb because you should never set a standard for
someone else that you can't reach.

You are *flawed, imperfect* and sometimes irrational but the same love
that covers your faults covers the faults of others. Be careful not to live
under grace and then *refuse* to extend it to others. I know that it takes
more energy and more patience to look beyond someone's mistakes and
love them anyway, but that's the example God has set. What example
are you setting? Today, love someone **IN SPITE OF**...yes, I'm talking to
YOU. Forgive again.

···

THE WORD:

*...for all have sinned and fall short of the glory of God, and are justified
freely by his grace through the redemption that came by Christ Jesus.
(Romans 3:23, 24 NIV84)*

*But because of his great love for us, God, who is rich in mercy, made us
alive with Christ even when we were dead in transgressions–it is by grace
you have been saved. (Ephesians 2:4, 5 NIV84)*

···

DAY TWENTY-ONE - THE WORK:

• *Name two people that you need to extend grace to this week.*

• *Choose one to contact today.*

_____

_____

_____

_____

_____

_____

_____

_____

_____

_____

_____

_____

_____

_____

_____

_____

_____

DAY TWENTY-TWO

· ·

No man knows the day or the hour...

· ·

THE WISDOM:

..so why do you live your life like you will always have time to correct what you did wrong and undo the mess you made in your **'I'm grown'** thought process? Stop taking advantage of God's grace by doing what **FEELS** good and **FEELS** right instead of doing what **IS** good and **IS** right.

You're spending too much time repenting and regretting because you make emotional decisions. I pray that you begin to make Spirit led decisions so that you can spend more time praising and progressing! Take the time to sow seeds of good decisions so that you can stop reaping a harvest of heartaches. You have a future filled with the promises of God. Go get it!

· ·

THE WORD:

Be very careful, then, how you live–not as unwise but as wise, making the most of every opportunity, because the days are evil. Therefore do not be foolish, but understand what the Lord's will is. (Ephesians 5:15-17 NIV84)

Teach us to realize the brevity of life, so that we may grow in wisdom. (Psalm 90:12 NLT)

· ·

DAY TWENTY-TWO - THE WORK:

- How have you taken advantage of God's grace?

- Name one way that you can move from making emotion led decisions to making Spirit led decisions.

- Commit to your change today.

_____

_____

_____

_____

_____

_____

_____

_____

_____

_____

_____

_____

_____

_____

DAY TWENTY-THREE

· ·

Sometimes *God uses circumstances to propel us into our purpose.*

· ·

THE WISDOM:

How many times have you walked away from an opportunity to help or denied the use of your gifts because you didn't think you were ready for the challenge?

We walk away from challenges for two reasons: fear of failure or fear of success. **Failure** brings disappointment. **Success** brings more responsibility; and we don't want either of the two. But lately God has been nudging you forward with circumstances and problems all around you. Do not give in to fear, activate your faith. Stop avoiding the issues. Step up to the challenge. Press through your problems. Your time has come.

Jesus knew that his divine purpose (the cross) hadn't come, but he also knew that this pivotal moment would push him to his destiny. Don't miss your moment. If God is presenting you with the problem and you have the ability to help, your time **FOR THIS** has come.

· ·

THE WORD:

When the wine was gone at the wedding, Jesus said "…"Woman, what does this have to do with me? My hour has not yet come." (John 2:4 ESV)

· ·

DAY TWENTY-THREE - THE WORK:

- *Are you more afraid of responsibility or disappointment?*

- *What opportunities are you avoiding because of fear?*

- *Pray for courage and face the challenge.*

_____

_____

_____

_____

_____

_____

_____

_____

_____

_____

_____

_____

_____

_____

_____

_____

_____

D A Y   T W E N T Y - F O U R

••

ME: **Ok God, what do you want me to tell your people today?**

GOD: **Stop walking away from me.**

••

THE WORD:

Stop walking away from God. Don't you hate when people you love walk away while you're talking? It's disrespectful and they obviously don't value what you're saying. Yet, we do it to God daily.

God is giving you direction, instructions and encouragement. Yet, you keep walking away to things and people who are more *"interesting"* than God. We walk away then complain that we don't think God hears us. He hears you, but allow me to encourage you to get closer so that you can hear Him. **God** loves you and He promised to never leave you. He's simply asking that you return the favor. There is a song with lyrics that ask, *"Why do I go astray when I know that I'm no good on my own?"* Receive this: God wants you near. You need God near. Stop walking away from God.

••

THE WORD:

Blessed are they whose ways are blameless, who walk according to the law of the Lord. (Psalm 119:1 NIV84)

But I gave them this command: Obey me, and I will be your God and you will be my people. Walk in all the ways I command you that it may go well with you. (Jeremiah 7:23 NIV84)

••

DAY TWENTY-FOUR - THE WORK:

- *How have you walked away from God in the past 30 days?*

- *Name a few of the things, places or people that distract you?*

- *Which are you willing to sacrifice to be closer to God?*

_____

_____

_____

_____

_____

_____

_____

_____

_____

_____

_____

_____

_____

_____

_____

DAY TWENTY-FIVE

··

You promised *that if He got you out of that last situation you* wouldn't *go back.*

··

THE WORD:

You worked really hard to be faithful and God was pleased. So what happened? How did you wind up here **again**? What or who keeps pushing you back to 'square one'? What or who is it in your life that's working against God's plans for you?

God appreciates that you take the responsibility to repent but you also need to reflect on why you keep making the same mistakes and falling into the same traps. He's already *set you free*. How did you get back into bondage? Repenting without reflection leads to repeating. My prayer for you today is that you take some time to check your <u>circle</u>, your <u>choices</u> and your <u>compromises</u>, so that when He sets you free this time, you'll STAY free. Don't get so frustrated that you stop trying. You can pass this test; you just have to do your homework. I'm praying for you.

··

THE WORD:

Stand fast therefore in the liberty by which Christ has made us free, and do not be entangled again with a yoke of bondage. (Galatians 5:1 NKJV)

You were running a good race. Who cut in on you and kept you from obeying the truth? That kind of persuasion does not come from the one who calls you. (Galatians 5:7, 8 NIV84)

··

DAY TWENTY-FIVE - THE WORK:

- _What or who contributes to your repeat mistakes?_

- _What are you compromising each time you give in to that behavioral choice?_

- _Name one way you can strengthen your resolve so that compromising in this area is no longer a choice._

_____

_____

_____

_____

_____

_____

_____

_____

_____

_____

_____

_____

_____

_____

DAY TWENTY-SIX

....

People say, *"The* truth hurts."

....

THE WISDOM:

A lie hurts too. It's just a delayed hurt. But why are you so mad that they keep lying? You haven't figured out that you're the one that keeps believing the lie? They (Satan included) lie to you, then you lie to yourself and the madness continues. **ENOUGH!**

You keep believing the same lie because you want to. The lie makes you feel better. The lie keeps you comfortable, but the lie keeps you bound and only the truth sets you free. Your truth and your trust are limited to your understanding. Your understanding of God's word, your understanding that you can't force people to change. You don't understand the truth so you don't trust it. Therefore, you keep settling for the lie. My prayer for you today is that you ask God for wisdom and a discerning spirit. **Seek the truth.** *Trust God. Don't believe the hype.*

....

THE WORD:
Wisdom is the principal thing; therefore get wisdom: and with all thy getting get understanding. (Proverbs 4:7 KJV)

Then you will know the truth, and the truth will set you free." (John 8:32 NIV84)
....

DAY TWENTY-SIX - THE WORD:

- *Is there a truth in your life that you continue to excuse or avoid?*

- *Why won't you trust or receive the truth that God is showing you?*

- *Pray for wisdom and discernment concerning this matter.*

- *As you gain clarity, record the thoughts in our journal so that in your weaker moments you can refer back to them for strength.*

_____

_____

_____

_____

_____

_____

_____

_____

_____

_____

_____

_____

_____

_____

_____

DAY TWENTY-SEVEN

....

Why do you continue to seek validation from people when God has already approved?

....

<u>THE WISDOM</u>:

God has given you your spot and your gifts will make room for you. So why do you keep doing things that scream for attention? Stop trying to impress people that have nothing to do with God's plan for you.

You are spiritually and emotionally competing against people that aren't even paying attention to you. You don't even realize how valuable you **ALREADY** are. You keep trying to strive to be this person that everybody loves and everybody needs. You even daydream of situations where you come out on top and people come back to say how wrong they were about you. You don't have time to be wrapped up in other's opinions of you. You are who God says you are. See yourself through your Father's eyes and allow His acceptance of you to release you from the traps of people-pleasing and approval addictions. My prayer for you today is that you realize this: *You are fearfully and wonderfully made*; handcrafted in the image of God. God loves you. I love you. And there is nothing you can do about it!

....

<u>THE WORD</u>:

I praise you because I am fearfully and wonderfully made; your works are wonderful, I know that full well. (Psalm 139:14 NIV84)

Whatever you do, work at it with all your heart, as working for the Lord, not for men, since you know that you will receive an inheritance from the Lord as a reward. It is the Lord Christ you are serving. (Colossians 3:23, 24 NIV84)

....

DAY TWENTY-SEVEN - THE WORK:

- *Find the best selfie of you in your phone. What quality makes it the best?*

- *Name three inner qualities that you love about yourself.*

- *Write positive affirmations using those three qualities to remind yourself that you are already God approved.*

- *Save them in your phone and refer to them three times today and as needed in the future.*

_____

_____

_____

_____

_____

_____

_____

_____

_____

_____

_____

_____

DAY TWENTY-EIGHT

....

You are loved.

....

THE WISDOM:

Don't allow the ups and downs of life and the stresses of finances or the fickleness of people make you question God's love. Elevate your thinking and stop confining God to man's behavior. God has never made you *earn* His love. Neither did He wait on you to deserve it. **God loves you unconditionally.**

You are so used to falling in and out of love that when you make a mistake you apologize to God like your relationship is probably over. You don't forgive yourself for bad decisions so you don't think God has forgiven you either. Then you make more bad decisions thinking that it doesn't matter anymore. It matters. *You matter.* Stop stacking your mistakes beside God's love thinking that as your stack increases His love decreases. That's what people do. But the God that we serve has a love that is consistent, dependable, steadfast, unmovable, and always abounding! In spite of where you've been, what you've done and who you did it with, **YOU ARE LOVED.** I pray that God reminds you throughout the day that His love still surrounds you, His grace still covers you and His mercy endures **FOREVER.**

THE WORD:

But God demonstrates his own love for us in this: While we were still sinners, Christ died for us. (Romans 5:8 NIV84)

But because of his great love for us, God, who is rich in mercy, made us alive with Christ even when we were dead in transgressions–it is by grace you have been saved. (Ephesians 2:4, 5 NIV84)

DAY TWENTY-EIGHT - THE WORK:

- *How do you know when someone loves you?*

- *What is written in God's word to let you know that He loves you?*

- *Write down what you want God to forgive you for, pray for forgiveness, and write the word GRACE over what you prayed for.*

- *Release it and receive God's forgiveness.*

_____

_____

_____

_____

_____

_____

_____

_____

_____

_____

_____

_____

_____

_____

DAY TWENTY-NINE

••

*There is **too much noise** in your life and it's causing you not to be able to hear **God's voice.***

••

THE WISDOM:

You stay in noisy places; you've got noisy friends that are always talking about nothing. You even have noisy habits (including social media). God wants you to spend some time **alone** but you don't like what you hear when it's quiet, so you go back to the noise.

See, in the noise we can talk to God but we don't have to listen. We can pretend to be Christ-like and say, *"I pray all the time,"* but if you're not listening to Him, you're not communicating with Him. Stop trying to hide in noise because you don't want to face who you've become, what you did or where you are. You are avoiding the voice of God because you know He's going to *ask you to change.* It's ok. Change is good. My prayer for you today is that you find that quiet place to hear God's voice. He's heard what you have to say, **now** it's time to listen to Him. He's whispering His will to you. He's whispering His purpose for you. **SSSHHH**... can you hear Him now?

•••

THE WORD:

The Lord said, "Go out and stand on the mountain in the presence of the Lord, for the Lord is about to pass by." Then a great and powerful wind tore the mountains apart and shattered the rocks before the Lord, but the Lord was not in the wind. After the wind there was an earthquake, but the Lord was not in the earthquake. After the earthquake came a fire, but the Lord was not in the fire. And after the fire came a gentle whisper. (1 Kings 19:11, 12 NIV84)

•••

DAY TWENTY-NINE - THE WORK:

- *What (or who) are the "noise-makers" in your life?*

- *Do you have trouble being alone or sitting quietly for extended periods of time?*

- *Today spend some quiet time with God. Suggestions: Take a walk without ear buds. Sit still for 30 minutes. Eat a meal alone without television or Internet.*

- *After your quiet time record your thoughts.*

_____

_____

_____

_____

_____

_____

_____

_____

_____

_____

_____

_____

D A Y   T H I R T Y

....

Speak Life.

....

THE WISDOM:

You can do this. I know it seems easier to give up right now but you can do this. I know it seems like nothing is working and everyone is against you, but you can do this. It **WILL** get better. This is **NOT** your end! Hold on! God says He is about to bless you **IN THE MIDDLE** of your storm. He is about to show up and show out.

God is going to open the door of opportunity and the window of blessings and allow the Holy Spirit to sweep through your life with fresh wind and fresh fire. Don't hold on to anything that the Holy Spirit is trying to sweep away. We tend to want to choose what stays and what leaves which means we have not completely surrendered. Surrender today so that God can bless you like He wants to. You think you know what you need and how you should be blessed - You have no clue. God is doing a new thing. Do you not perceive it? Stay faithful and watch God blow your mind!

THE WORD:

When the storm has swept by, the wicked are gone, but the righteous stand firm forever. (Proverbs 10:25 NIV84)

"Forget the former things; do not dwell on the past. See, I am doing a new thing! Now it springs up; do you not perceive it? I am making a way in the desert and streams in the wasteland. (Isaiah 43:18, 19 NIV84)

DAY THIRTY - THE WORK:

- *Name your goal.*

- *What are the benefits of reaching your goal?*

- *Use the benefits you listed to formulate positive affirmations that will speak life into your "new thing."*

_____

_____

_____

_____

_____

_____

_____

_____

_____

_____

_____

_____

_____

DAY THIRTY-ONE

....
Getting on the soapbox
....

THE WISDOM:

What are you waiting on to **START** your dream? You're wasting time.
How can you publish a book without writing the first sentence? You've
been talking about a nonprofit to help people for three years and you
don't even know where to find the 501(c) 3 paperwork. **SMH!** (If you
don't want to hear me fuss, stop reading now)

You've told everybody that "I'm supposed to do this" or "I'm going to
be that" and you're mad because they don't believe you. Why are you
surprised that they don't believe in you? You don't even *believe in you!*
Then you want to jump up and wave your hand when the preacher
says "You can't tell everybody your dreams" Chile please! Ain't nobody
blocking you but YOU.

And quit talking about people hating on you. Your haters are currently
unemployed cause you ain't doing nothing for them to hate.

The devil said you couldn't do it. Stop **SAYING** he's a lie and **MAKE**
him one! If God gave you the desire, He is more than able to fulfill it.
Just start. Take the first step. Write the first sentence. **YOU CAN DO
THIS!!!**

I decree it. I declare it. I call it forth in the Spirit - you will become what
God designed you to be! **MANIFEST!**

Believe. Achieve. Receive.

DAY THIRTY-ONE - THE WORK:

- *What should you be doing right now with your life that you aren't doing?*

- *Have you written a plan?*

- *Do you believe in yourself? Do you believe in your plan? Do you believe God?*

- *Make the answers to these questions YES and watch your works begin to match your faith.*

_____

_____

_____

_____

_____

_____

_____

_____

_____

_____

_____

_____

_____

_____

DAY THIRTY-TWO

··

What are you afraid of?

··

THE WISDOM:

You've heard from God on the situation. You've even asked Him a couple of times to repeat what He said and you **STILL** haven't stepped out on faith. I repeat: *What are you afraid of?*

You **CAN** defeat the *fear* that tries to stop you, block you or keep you stagnant because *you are* more than a conqueror through Him that loves you. You have access to an all-powerful God. Today I pray that you bind fear and release courage; bind uncertainty and release boldness. Courage is not the absence of fear. Courage is doing it afraid. Let today be **YOUR** day. Start your plan and plan to finish. *Greatness awaits you.* On your mark, get set, GO!

THE WORD:

No, in all these things we are more than conquerors through him who loved us. (Romans 8:37 NIV84)

For God has not given us a spirit of fear, but of power and of love and of a sound mind. (2 Timothy 1:7 NKJV)

DAY THIRTY-TWO - THE WORK:

- *What would you do if you weren't afraid?*

- *Write it down. Each time you think of it or speak of it, recite 2 Timothy 1:7 until your plan is accomplished.*

_____

_____

_____

_____

_____

_____

_____

_____

_____

_____

_____

_____

_____

_____

_____

_____

DAY THIRTY-THREE

....

These were my thoughts this morning.

....

THE WISDOM:

I pray it gives *you hope*. If you are at the end of your rope, tie a knot and hold on because...

God hears. God heals. God answers. God anchors. God loves. God lifts. God supports. God satisfies. God restores. God reaches. God promises. God delivers. God helps. God holds. God sustains. God saves. God keeps. God covers. God blocks. God builds. God stops. God saves. God pushes. God pulls. God forgives. God favors. God mends. God moves. **GOD IS**.

Don't give up the fight. Your breakthrough is nearer than you think. I'm praying for you.

....

THE WORD:

Let us hold unswervingly to the hope we profess, for he who promised is faithful. (Hebrews 10:23 NIV84)

For I am the Lord, your God, who takes hold of your right hand and says to you, Do not fear; I will help you. (Isaiah 41:13 NIV84)

....

DAY THIRTY-THREE - THE WORK:

- *Pick out three of the God affirmations above that bring hope to your current situation.*

- *Complete this sentence: I still have hope because* _____
  _____

- *Do this throughout the day to change your thought process and your attitude.*

_____

_____

_____

_____

_____

_____

_____

_____

_____

_____

_____

_____

DAY THIRTY-FOUR

....

You were handmade, handcrafted and handpicked for your destiny.

....

THE WISDOM:

It is **YOUR** destiny - a gift from God. The enemy has no power to take your destiny so he's trying to convince you to give up. Read this twice: The only person that can stop you is **YOU**.

You may not be the best, the smartest, or the fastest but *God chooses ordinary people* to do *extraordinary* things. It may not make sense, people may laugh and even you don't understand; but trust and believe, God chose **YOU**. God believes in **YOU**. God will provide for **YOU**. He does not always call the equipped but He always equips the called. *Surrender your doubt and move toward your destiny.* I'm praying for you .

THE WORD:

But God chose the foolish things of the world to shame the wise; God chose the weak things of the world to shame the strong. He chose the lowly things of this world and the despised things–and the things that are not–to nullify the things that are, (1 Corinthians 1:27, 28 NIV84)

DAY THIRTY-FOUR - THE WORK:

- How are you blocking or delaying your destiny?

- How is God equipping you for your future?

- Begin to pray against all doubt, fear or excuses.

_____

_____

_____

_____

_____

_____

_____

_____

_____

_____

_____

_____

_____

_____

DAY THIRTY-FIVE

....

Every time you meet someone new and in every other social media post you say **how special and how different you are from the rest.**

....

THE WISDOM:

Yet, you keep having a crowd mentality and making crowd decisions. Are you trying to convince us or trying to convince yourself? Are we supposed to believe **what you know** or **what you show?**

There is something about you that makes you different; something on the inside that makes you standout. *God has placed the light of His love in you and the light of His favor upon you.* But every time you settle for things beneath His will, your light gets dimmer. Every time you try to hide who you are in Him to fit in with the crowd, your light gets dimmer. Stop dumbing down, blending in, covering up, hiding under and getting over. You can't SHINE like that and you can't LEAD from the middle of the pack. As a matter of fact, the people that you're running with are moving too slowly for you. Step out of the pack and set the pace for the race God had designed for you. You were not created to fit in. YOU were created to stand out. Let your light SHINE!

....

THE WORD:

Therefore, since we are surrounded by such a great cloud of witnesses, let us throw off everything that hinders and the sin that so easily entangles, and let us run with perseverance the race marked out for us. (Hebrews 12:1 NIV84)

For you were once darkness, but now you are light in the Lord. Live as children of light (Ephesians 5:8 NIV84)

In the same way, let your light shine before men, that they may see your good deeds and praise your Father in heaven. (Matthew 5:16 NIV84)

....

DAY THIRTY-FIVE - THE WORK:

- *What makes you different?*

- *How can you embrace your differences and stop downplaying who you were created to be?*

- *Post a selfie today with these hashtags: #ImDifferent #FearfullyandWonderfullyMade*

_____

_____

_____

_____

_____

_____

_____

_____

_____

_____

_____

_____

_____

DAY THIRTY-SIX

••

There are people in your life *that you are expecting* more from *than they can deliver.*

••

THE WISDOM:

And every time they miss the **mark** you lose your mind. Face it. They are *being* who they are and you want more for them than they want for themselves. People rarely disappoint us, *our expectations of people disappoint us.*

The enemy uses unrealistic expectations to steal our joy and destroy our peace. God **alone** is perfect. *Everyone* else is under construction including you! Put your faith in God, pray for them and forgive them. One day you'll need forgiveness too :)

My hope is built on nothing less
Than Jesus' blood and righteousness;
I dare not trust the sweetest frame,
But wholly lean on Jesus' name.
~Excerpt from the Hymn: 'On Christ the Solid Rock I Stand'

••

THE WORD:

For if you forgive other people when they sin against you, your heavenly Father will also forgive you. But if you do not forgive others their sins, your Father will not forgive your sins. (Matthew 6:14-15 NIV)

Do not judge others, and you will not be judged. Do not condemn others, or it will all come back against you. Forgive others, and you will be forgiven. (Luke 6:37 NLT)

••

DAY THIRTY-SIX - THE WORK:

- *Who are you disappointed in because they did not meet your expectations?*

- *Did they agree to the expectations?*

- *How many times have you agreed to God's expectations and fell short?*

- *Pray for them and extend the same grace to them that God has extended to you.*

_____

_____

_____

_____

_____

_____

_____

_____

_____

_____

_____

_____

DAY THIRTY-SEVEN

··

I often hear people say,
"I have no idea what I'm supposed to do."

··

THE WISDOM:

But in your case, God has not only given you a *desire* for more, He has given you a desire for better. He has even **given** you an avenue (idea) on how to achieve it. All you have to do is *plan and focus* so please stop trying to sound *"holy,"* talking about you're waiting on God when God is really waiting on **YOU!**

So what's the delay? Why haven't you done your part? You keep praying for God to make a way, to open doors. The way has been made and the door is open. **DO THE WORK** so you can get the blessing! Stop walking outside with a bowl, waiting on manna to fall from the sky. God put the manna seed of provision in your head. Now, do you have the *heart to plant* it so that you can **reap** your harvest? I believe that you do. I'm praying for you.

THE WORD:

9 For this reason, since the day we heard about you, we have not stopped praying for you. We continually ask God to fill you with the knowledge of his will through all the wisdom and understanding that the Spirit gives, 10 so that you may live a life worthy of the Lord and please him in every way: bearing fruit in every good work, growing in the knowledge of God, 11 being strengthened with all power according to his glorious might so that you may have great endurance and patience, 12 and giving joyful thanks to the Father, who has qualified you to share in the inheritance of his holy people in the kingdom of light. (Colossians 1:9-12 NIV)

DAY THIRTY-SEVEN - THE WORK:

- Go back through this journal and look at the plans you have written.

- Have you done what you said you would do? Why or why not?

- What has been your delay? Don't revise the plan. DO THE WORK!

_____

_____

_____

_____

_____

_____

_____

_____

_____

_____

_____

_____

_____

_____

D A Y T H I R T Y - E I G H T

....

God knows *what you need.*

....

THE WISDOM:

God also knows when you need it. What you are asking for is not a surprise to Him, it didn't catch Him off guard. He's not scrambling to figure out how to respond to you. No ma'am! No Sir! He knew *before* you did and He's preparing you for your blessing.

You're asking for deliverance or asking for a mate and you think He's not listening. But through this storm, He's giving you the faith that you will need **AFTER** He delivers you. In your singleness, He's developing the character and patience you will need **AFTER** you get married. If He gave it to you now, you'd jack it up and He'd have to come to the rescue...*again.*

My prayer for you today is that you don't try to get out of this prematurely. Let God do His work so that you become *mature and complete* - not lacking anything.

....

THE WORD:

...because you know that the testing of your faith develops perseverance. Perseverance must finish its work so that you may be mature and complete, not lacking anything. (James 1:3, 4 NIV84)

Blessed is the man who perseveres under trial, because when he has stood the test, he will receive the crown of life that God has promised to those who love him. (James 1:12 NIV84)

DAY THIRTY-EIGHT - THE WORK:

- *What prayer concern has resurfaced repeatedly during your completion of this journal?*

- *If you have "done the work" that God has required, what characteristic(s) do you believe God is attempting to work in you or out of you during this holding pattern?*

- *Pray for those things to be revealed as you persevere.*

_____

_____

_____

_____

_____

_____

_____

_____

_____

_____

_____

_____

_____

DAY THIRTY-NINE

....

*You **prayed** for God to heal you,
help you, fix you and finish you,...*

....

THE WISDOM:

...and nothing has changed for you. You believe that God is able to do *anything*. You're just not sure if He is *willing* to do it for you. Allow me to encourage you with this: No matter what you've done, where you've been or who you've "been there and done it" with, God's forgiveness is available. His *grace and mercy* is available. He still loves you.

You are not what you did! The way you see **YOU** is not an accurate picture of what Christ has done for you. God **wants** you back. He wants to restore you back to your rightful place with Him. **YES, HE WILL GIVE YOU ANOTHER CHANCE**, but will you take it? I pray that you do. Cleanse your conscience and *receive* God's **grace** today.

....

THE WORD:

Let us therefore come boldly to the throne of grace, that we may obtain mercy and find grace to help in time of need. (Hebrews 4:16 NKJV)

How much more, then, will the blood of Christ, who through the eternal Spirit offered himself unblemished to God, cleanse our consciences from acts that lead to death, so that we may serve the living God! (Hebrews 9:14 NIV)

....

DAY THIRTY-NINE - THE WORD:

- *In what area of your life are you requesting a second chance?*

- *Take the time today to write a prayer regarding your request and include Hebrews 4:16. Read it throughout the day and before you end your evening.*

_____

_____

_____

_____

_____

_____

_____

_____

_____

_____

_____

_____

_____

_____

D A Y   F O R T Y

"Shake well before use. Contents may settle."

THE WISDOM:

God is getting ready to use you for His glory but you don't think you have what it takes. This season of turmoil will bring out the best in you, including the *confidence* you need to have *victory* in your next season.

God has already placed **everything** inside of you that you need to fulfill your purpose. However, when things look hard or uncomfortable we tend to settle for what's easy or choose the path of least resistance. This is why God has to shake us and allow trouble in our lives. Then the *faith, perseverance and power* that are already in us will begin to rise to the surface and God shows us what we're made of. You **CAN** handle this situation. You **CAN** handle this season. My prayer for you today is that you let your spiritual content rise during this storm and don't settle for less than God promised you. Get ready for God's glory to be revealed! You're about see what you're **REALLY** made of. I'm excited for you.

THE WORD:

And the God of all grace, who called you to his eternal glory in Christ, after you have suffered a little while, will himself restore you and make you strong, firm and steadfast. (1 Peter 5:10 NIV84)

In this you greatly rejoice, though now for a little while you may have had to suffer grief in all kinds of trials. These have come so that your faith–of greater worth than gold, which perishes even though refined by fire–may be proved genuine and may result in praise, glory and honor when Jesus Christ is revealed. (1 Peter 1:6, 7 NIV84)

DAY FORTY - THE WORK:

- *What areas of your life are the most challenging right now?*

- *Why do you think these are the areas that you are struggling with in this season of your life?*

- *Ask your inner circle to begin to pray for your endurance as you face the challenges and God reveals what you are made of.*

_____

_____

_____

_____

_____

_____

_____

_____

_____

_____

_____

_____

_____

_____

HOW THIS JOURNAL CAN HELP

After reading this journal as a daily devotional, you may also use it as a continual reference by choosing topics based on your current need.

CHECK YOURSELF | DAYS: *7, 8, 15, 17, 22, 24, 25, 27, 26 & 37*

ENCOURAGEMENT | DAY: *9*

ENDURANCE | DAYS: *11, 13, 16, 30, 32, 33, 40 & 38*

FAITH | DAYS: *5, 10, 13, 18, 32 & 38*

FORGIVENESS | DAYS: *6, 19, 21, 25, 28, 39 & 36*

HEARING FROM GOD | DAYS: *4, 10 & 29*

OBEDIENCE | DAYS: *7, 8, 15, 24 & 37*

PAST | DAYS: *1 & 6*

PEACE | DAYS: *5 & 8*

PURPOSE | DAYS: *9, 12, 13, 14, 20, 23, 27, 31, 34, 35 & 40*

WISDOM | DAYS: *12 & 26*

ABOUT THE AUTHOR

Dynamic speaker, Powerful Motivator, and Certified Professional Coach; Karren Todd is a native Memphian with over 20 years of experience in leadership development and team dynamics. Fusing her gift of humor with world class coaching techniques, Karren helps her clients digest the hard truths so that they can SEE more, DO more and BE more.

After serving 15 years in full time ministry, with eight years as Senior Associate Pastor of New Direction Christian Church, Karren is now walking fully in her entrepreneurial gifts and continues to serve God by serving others. She is the Executive Director of POWER Ministries –a nonprofit that empowers women and girls to discover and unleash God's power that is within them. She has launched powerful initiatives such as Project STAND –an initiative that seeks to help raise awareness and resources for survivors and those surviving domestic violence; and Higher Learning which blends life skills, self-esteem, emotional intelligence and conflict resolution to prepare teen girls to be productive in their schools and communities.

Loving mother and community advocate, Karren completed her Master of Divinity from Memphis Theological Seminary in Spring 2017 and has been accepted in the Doctor of Ministry program for Pastoral Therapy. She has received many honors and awards including Women of Excellence and Female Pastor of the Year and Karren currently serves on the Board of Directors for Leadership Memphis.

To contact the author or to request for a speaking engagement, please visit: *www.karrentodd.com* or email: *success@coachkarren.com.*

Made in the USA
Columbia, SC
22 April 2023

15339729R00075